SECOND EDITION

TOUCHSTONE

WORKBOOK 1B

MICHAEL MCCARTHY
JEANNE MCCARTEN
HELEN SANDIFORD

CAMBRIDGE
UNIVERSITY PRESS

University Printing House, Cambridge CB2 8BS, United Kingdom

One Liberty Plaza, 20th Floor, New York, NY 10006, USA

477 Williamstown Road, Port Melbourne, VIC 3207, Australia

314–321, 3rd Floor, Plot 3, Splendor Forum, Jasola District Centre, New Delhi – 110025, India

103 Penang Road, #05-06/07, Visioncrest Commercial, Singapore 238467

Cambridge University Press is part of the University of Cambridge.

It furthers the University's mission by disseminating knowledge in the pursuit of education, learning and research at the highest international levels of excellence.

www.cambridge.org
Information on this title: www.cambridge.org/9781107691254

© Cambridge University Press 2005, 2014

This publication is in copyright. Subject to statutory exception and to the provisions of relevant collective licensing agreements, no reproduction of any part may take place without the written permission of Cambridge University Press.

First published 2005
Second Edition 2014

20 19 18 17 16 15 14 13 12 11 10 9 8

Printed in Great Britain by CPI Group (UK) Ltd, Croydon CR0 4YY

A catalog record for this publication is available from the British Library.

ISBN 978-1-107-67987-0 Student's Book
ISBN 978-1-107-62792-5 Student's Book A
ISBN 978-1-107-65345-0 Student's Book B
ISBN 978-1-107-63933-1 Workbook
ISBN 978-1-107-67071-6 Workbook A
ISBN 978-1-107-69125-4 Workbook B
ISBN 978-1-107-68330-3 Full Contact
ISBN 978-1-107-66769-3 Full Contact A
ISBN 978-1-107-61366-9 Full Contact B
ISBN 978-1-107-64223-2 Teacher's Edition with Assessment Audio CD/CD-ROM
ISBN 978-1-107-61414-7 Class Audio CDs (4)

Additional resources for this publication at www.cambridge.org/touchstone2

Cambridge University Press has no responsibility for the persistence or accuracy of URLs for external or third-party internet websites referred to in this publication, and does not guarantee that any content on such websites is, or will remain, accurate or appropriate. Information regarding prices, travel timetables, and other factual information given in this work is correct at the time of first printing but Cambridge University Press does not guarantee the accuracy of such information thereafter.

Contents

7 Out and about 50

8 Shopping..... 58

9 A wide world 66

10 Busy lives 74

11 Looking back 82

12 Fabulous food 90

Out and about

UNIT 7

Lesson A Away for the weekend

1 What's the weather like?

Vocabulary **A Write two sentences about each picture.**

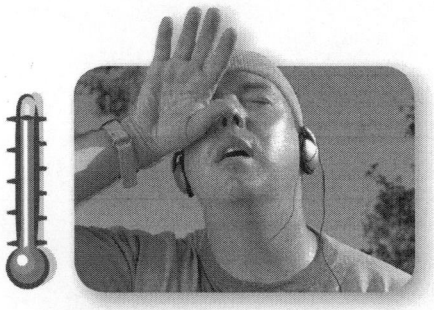

1. *It's hot.*
   It's sunny.

2. _____

3. _____

4. _____

5. _____

6. _____

B Answer the questions. Write true answers.

1. How many seasons do you have in your city? What are they? _____
2. What's your favorite season? Why? _____
3. What kind of weather do you like? Cold weather? Hot weather? _____
4. What's the weather like today? Is it warm? _____
5. What's the weather usually like at this time of year? _____
6. Does it ever snow in your city? If yes, when? _____

2 I'm waiting for a friend.

Grammar **Complete the conversation. Use the present continuous.**

Erin Hi, Ken. It's Erin. Where are you?

Ken Oh, hi, Erin. I'm at the beach. I *'m spending* (spend) the day with Tom. It's beautiful here today! It's, uh . . .

Erin Nice. . . . I'm so happy you _____ (have) fun.

Ken Yeah. We _____ (relax). We _____ (not do) anything special – I mean, I _____ (read) a book, and Tom _____ (swim). How about you? Are you at work?

Erin No. I _____ (not work) today.

Ken Oh, right. So, where – oops! Uh, I'm sorry. I _____ (eat) ice cream. I'm starving.

Erin Yeah, me too. I _____ (eat) a cookie.

Ken Really? So, where are you? I mean, are you at home?

Erin No, I'm at Pierre's Café. I _____ (wait) for a friend. He's very late.

Ken Oh, really? Who?

Erin You!

3 About you

Grammar and vocabulary **Are these sentences true or false for you right now? Write *T* (true) or *F* (false). Then correct the false sentences.**

1. *F* I'm eating dinner right now.
   I'm not eating dinner right now. I'm doing my homework.
2. ____ I'm using a computer.
   _____
3. ____ My family is watching TV.
   _____
4. ____ My friends are working.
   _____
5. ____ It's snowing.
   _____
6. ____ My best friend is skiing.
   _____

Lesson B Sports and exercise

1 All about sports

Vocabulary **A** **Write the names of the sports or kinds of exercise under the pictures.**

1. *volleyball*

2. _____

3. _____

4. _____

5. _____

6. _____

7. _____

8. _____

9. _____

B **Complete the chart with the words in part A.**

People play . . .	People do . . .	People go . . .
volleyball		

C **Answer the questions. Write true answers.**

1. What sports do you play? How often? *I play volleyball on Wednesdays and basketball on the weekends.*
2. What sports do your friends play? _____
3. Do you ever go biking? _____
4. What sports do people in your country like? _____

2 What are you doing?

Grammar **Complete the conversations with present continuous questions.**

1. **Joe** Hey, Luis! *What are you doing* (What / you / do) ?
   Are you at home?
   Luis No, I'm at the park. I'm playing tennis.
   Joe Really? _____ (you / play)
   with Janet?
   Luis No, I'm playing with John today.
   Joe Oh. So, _____ (you / have / fun) ?
   Luis No, I'm not. You know, it's raining here, and it's cold.
   Joe That's too bad. _____ (you / play)
   right now? In the rain?
   Luis Yes, we are. And it's my turn to serve. Hold on a minute. . . .
   Joe So, um, _____ (you / win) ?
   Luis Uh, no. I'm not playing very well today.
   Joe Is it because you're talking on your
   cell phone?

2. **Janet** Hi, Kelly. _____ (How / you / do) ?
   Kelly Hi. Great. How are you? _____ (you / work)
   this summer?
   Janet Yes, I'm working at a gym. I'm teaching there. It's fun.
   Kelly Really? _____ (What / you / teach) ?
   Janet Aerobics.
   Kelly Cool. So, _____ (you / do) other things?
   I mean, _____ (you / swim), too?
   Janet Yeah. There's a pool at the gym. So, _____
   (you / do) anything special this summer?
   Kelly Well, no. I'm living in my sister's apartment. She's in
   San Francisco this summer.
   Janet Really? _____ (What / she / do)
   there?
   Kelly She's working in a restaurant.
   Janet _____ (she / meet) a lot of
   new people?
   Kelly Oh, yes. She's having a good time.

1 Keep the conversation going!

Conversation strategies **Complete the conversation with the follow-up questions in the box.**

Where are you working?	✓What are you doing?
Are you practicing your languages?	So, why are you studying Spanish and Portuguese?
What classes are you taking?	Are you enjoying your classes?

Alex Hey, Kate. How's it going?

Kate Good. How are things with you?

Alex Great. But I'm really busy this summer.

Kate Really? *What are you doing?*

Alex Well, I'm taking a couple of classes, and I'm working.

Kate Wow! You're working and studying? _____

Alex I'm taking Spanish and Portuguese.

Kate That's interesting. _____

Alex Yeah, I really am. I'm learning a lot!

Kate That's great. _____

Alex Well, I'm thinking about a trip to South America.

Kate That's exciting!

Alex Yeah, and that's why I'm working two jobs, you know.

Kate Right. _____

Alex Well, I'm working at a Peruvian restaurant from 11:00 to 5:00, and I'm working at a Brazilian music club at night.

Kate Really? Wow! _____

Alex Yes, I am! I'm speaking Spanish all day and Portuguese all night.

Kate That's really cool! But when do you sleep?

Alex That's a problem. Sometimes I sleep in class.

Kate Oh, right. That *is* a problem.

2 Asking follow-up questions

Conversation strategies **Complete two follow-up questions for each comment.**

1. "I don't play sports, but I often go running with a friend."

   Really? Where *do you go running* ?
   How often _____ ?

2. "My parents are on vacation this month."

   That's nice. Where _____ ?
   Are they _____ ?

3. "My grandparents are visiting this week."

   Really? Where _____ ?
   How often _____ ?

4. "I'm working nights this summer."

   Really? Where _____ ?
   What time _____ ?

3 Oh, that's good.

Conversation strategies **Read these people's comments about their summer activities. Complete the responses. Then ask follow-up questions.**

1. I'm really enjoying my vacation this summer.

   Oh, that's *good* .
   What are you doing ?

2. I'm not doing anything exciting. I'm just reading a lot.

   That's _____ .
   _____ ?

3. I'm not enjoying this summer at all. I'm working ten hours a day.

   Really? That's _____ .
   _____ ?

4. I'm just relaxing, and I'm watching a lot of TV.

   Hey, that's _____ .
   _____ ?

5. I'm exercising a lot at the gym this summer.

   That's _____ .
   _____ ?

6. What vacation? I'm painting my house right now.

   Really? That's _____ .
   _____ ?

Lesson D Staying in shape

1 An advice column

Reading **A Which sports and exercises do you do? Check (✓) the boxes.**

☐ aerobics ☐ biking ☐ skiing ☐ volleyball
☐ basketball ☐ running ☐ soccer ☐ weight training

B Read the advice column. Match the problems with the Sports Professional's advice.

FITNESS TALK

Do you have a question about exercise? Write to Steven, the Sports Professional, for help and good advice.

1. **John:** I never exercise. I drive to work, and I sit all day. I hate sports, and I don't like the gym. I know it's a good idea to exercise, but how do I start? _____

2. **Amy:** I'm really busy this year. I'm going to school, and I'm working part-time at night. I like exercise, but I don't have a lot of time. Help! _____

3. **Bill:** I do weight training at the gym every day. I usually love exercise, but these days, it's boring. I think I need a break. What do you think?

a. **The Sports Professional:** Slowly add exercise to your weekly routine. Walk or ride a bike to work – don't drive. Use the stairs, not the elevator. Clean the house, or do the laundry. Just do something – and start today!

b. **The Sports Professional:** You're right. You need a break. Try exergaming for a change. There are a lot of different types of activities, and each one helps your body in a different way. Don't stop your weight training, and remember, running is always good for you, too.

c. **The Sports Professional:** Yes, I know the problem, but try and make time. Experts say we need 30 minutes of exercise five times a week. So, do aerobics for 15 minutes in the morning. Go to school. Then go running for 15 minutes in the evening after work.

C Read the advice column again. Then answer the questions.

1. Is John getting enough exercise these days? _____
2. Does John like sports? _____
3. Amy is busy this year. What is she doing? _____
4. What is Amy's problem? _____
5. How often does Bill go to the gym? _____
6. What does Bill do at the gym? _____

2 Write your own advice.

Writing **A** **Look again at the advice column on page 56. Find two imperatives the Sports Professional uses in each piece of advice.**

Try exergaming for a change.

B **Make imperatives for advice. Match the verbs with the words and expressions.**

(Don't)	be	aerobics in the morning	*Don't be shy.*
	buy	at least five times a week	*Buy some good running shoes.*
	do	shy	
	drive	some good running shoes	
	exercise	to work	
	watch	TV all the time	

C **Read the problems. Reply to each person. Give two pieces of advice using imperatives. Use the ideas above or your own ideas.**

1. **Joe:** I watch sports on TV all the time. I'm watching the Olympics this month. It's great, but I don't do any sports. What sports are fun?
   The Sports Professional: *Try a lot of different sports. I like volleyball, tennis, and swimming. Also,* _____

2. **Anita:** This fall, we're playing soccer at school. I'm not enjoying it very much, especially when it's cold! Also, I'm not very good. Help!
   The Sports Professional: _____

3. **David:** I like exercise, but I'm lazy! I usually exercise for two or three weeks, but then I need a break. Do you have any advice?
   The Sports Professional: _____

Unit 7 Progress chart

	What can you do? Mark the boxes. ✓ = I can . . . ? = I need to review how to . . .	To review, go back to these pages in the Student's Book.
Grammar	☐ make present continuous statements. ☐ ask present continuous questions.	66 and 67 68 and 69
Vocabulary	☐ name at least 6 words to talk about the weather. ☐ name at least 10 sports and kinds of exercise.	65, 66, and 67 67 and 68
Conversation strategies	☐ ask follow-up questions to keep the conversation going. ☐ react to things people say with *That's . . .* expressions.	70 and 71 71
Writing	☐ use imperatives to give instructions and advice.	73

Shopping

UNIT 8

Lesson A Clothes

1 Do a crossword puzzle.

Vocabulary **A** Complete the crossword puzzle. Write the names of the clothes.

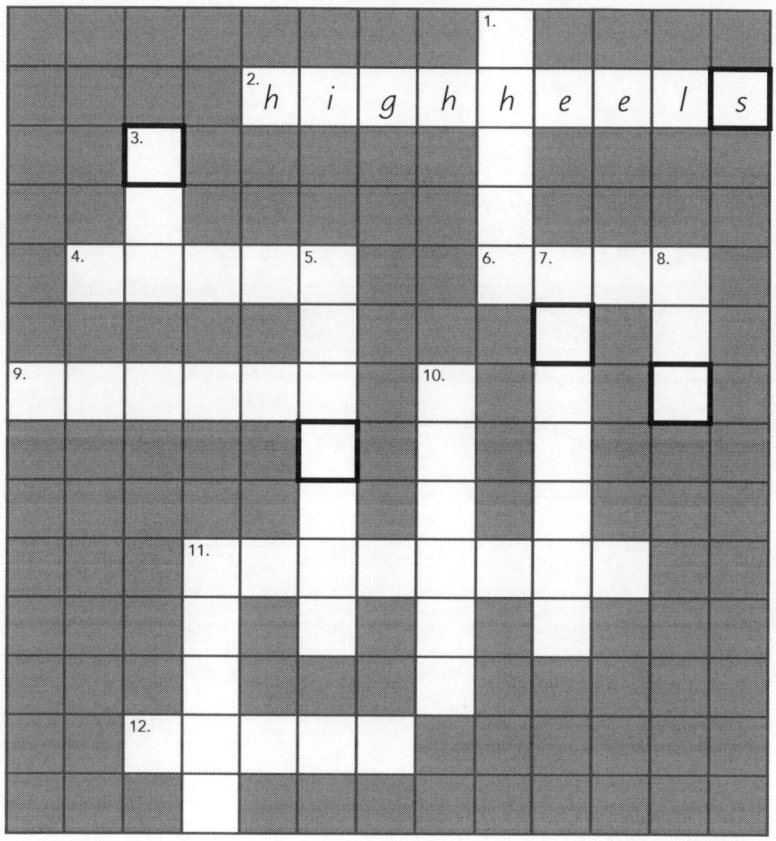

Down

1. 

3. 

5. 

7. 

8. 

10. 

11. 

Across

2. 

4. 

6. 

9. 

11. 

12. 

B Now find the five highlighted letters in the puzzle. What do they spell?

____ ____ ____ ____ s

2 I want to spend some money!

Grammar **Complete the conversations with the correct form of the verbs.**

1. **Mia** Let's go shopping. I *need to buy* (need / buy) some new clothes.
   Rick OK. Where do you _____ (want / go) ?
   Mia To the mall. I _____ (need / get) some new jeans. And I _____ (have / get) a couple of new suits for work.
   Rick Listen. You go. I think I _____ (want / stay) home. I _____ (not need / buy) anything, and I _____ (want / check) my email.
   Mia OK!

2. **Will** I have a date with Megan tonight. She _____ (want / go) to an expensive restaurant.
   Ana Really? Do you have any good clothes? Those old jeans are terrible. And you know Megan – she _____ (like / wear) designer clothes.
   Will I know, but I _____ (like / wear) my jeans! And I _____ (not want / go) to a restaurant anyway. I _____ (want / go) to a movie.
   Ana Oh, there's the phone. Hello? . . . Will, it's Megan. She's sick.
   Will Oh, no! Well, now I _____ (not have / change) my clothes!

3 About you

Grammar and vocabulary **Unscramble the questions. Then write true answers.**

1. A to the movies / do / like / What / to / wear / you ? *What do you like to wear to the movies?*
   B _____
2. A nice / have / When / do / to / clothes / you / wear ? _____
   B _____
3. A you / Do / a / have / uniform / to / wear ? _____
   B _____
4. A buy / Do / like / you / to / online / things ? _____
   B _____
5. A clothes / do / What / want / you / buy / to ? _____
   B _____
6. A do / go / like / Where / you / to / shopping ? _____
   B _____

Lesson B Things to buy

1 Accessories

Vocabulary **Write the words under the pictures using *a* or *some*.**

1. *some jeans*

2. *a dress*

3. _____

4. _____

5. _____

6. _____

7. _____

8. _____

9. _____

10. _____

11. _____

12. _____

13. _____

14. _____

15. _____

16. _____

2 Colors

Vocabulary **Complete the color words in the box. Then answer the questions, and complete the chart. Write three colors to answer each question, if possible.**

r*e*d y_____w b_____k p_____e w_____e
o_____e b_____e g_____n b_____n g_____y

What colors . . .			
do you like to wear?	*blue*		
are you wearing right now?			
do you never wear?			
are in your home?			
are your favorites?			
are popular right now?			
are in your country's flag?			

3 How much is this?

Grammar **A Complete the conversations. Use *this, that, these,* or *those*.**

1. **Lena** Um, excuse me. How much is *that* dress?
   Clerk The red dress? It's $325.
   Lena Oh. And how about _____ shoes?
   Clerk They're $149.
   Lena Oh, really. And what about _____ T-shirts? Are they expensive, too?
   Clerk They're $49.
   Lena Oh, well. Thanks anyway.

2. **Tito** Excuse me.
   Seller Yes?
   Tito How much are _____ umbrellas?
   Seller They're $19.99.
   Tito $19.99? Really?
   Seller Oh, wait. Sorry. _____ umbrella is $4.99. _____ umbrellas over here are $19.99.
   Tito OK, so I want _____ umbrella, please.

B Look at the pictures. Write questions and answers.

1. 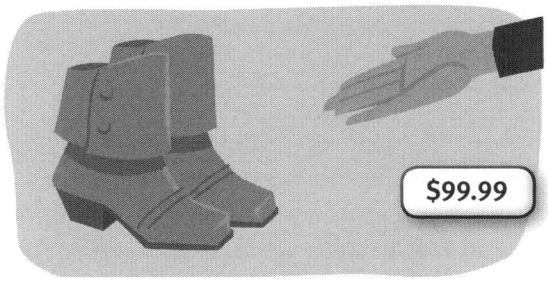

   A *How much are those boots?*
   B _____

2. 

   A _____
   B _____

3. 

   A _____
   B _____

4. 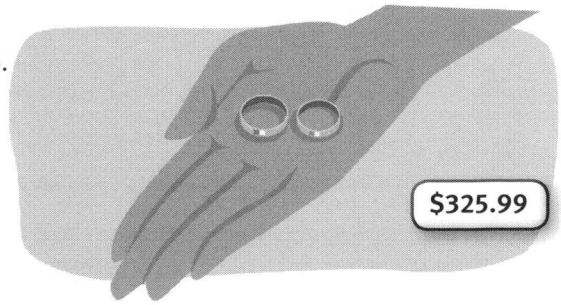

   A _____
   B _____

Lesson C Can I help you?

1 Um, uh, oh!

Conversation strategies

Complete the chart with the "conversation sounds" and expressions in the box.

✓I know.	Let's see.	Really?	Uh,	Um,	Yeah.
Let me think.	Oh.	Right.	Uh-huh.	Well,	

You want to show you agree.	You are surprised.	You need time to think.
I know.		

2 About you

Conversation strategies

Answer the questions with true information. Start each answer with a "time to think" expression.

1. What's your favorite color?

   Let me think. . . . I guess it's green.

2. What's your favorite thing to wear?

   _____

3. How often do you shop online?

   _____

4. How much do jeans cost these days?

   _____

5. How many birthday presents do you have to buy this month?

   _____

6. Does your family like to shop for clothes together?

   _____

3 Are you listening?

Conversation strategies **Complete the conversation with the correct expressions.**

Roberto Mom, I have to get some things for college.

Mother _____ What do you need to get?
(Uh-huh. / Let me think.)

Roberto _____ . . . I need to get a new computer and . . .
(Um, let's see. / Really!)

Mother _____ They're expensive.
(Let me think. / Oh, really?)

Roberto I know. But I have to go online a lot for my classes.

Mother Well, OK. And what else do you want?

Roberto _____ I want to get a new cell phone and . . .
(Uh-huh. / Uh, well . . .)

Mother _____ I'm surprised. I mean,
(Oh, / Um,)
you usually don't call, so . . .

Roberto Well, I text sometimes. Anyway, _____ Oh, yes, and
(let's see. / uh-huh.)
I have to get some new sneakers.

Mother _____ You really need new sneakers. Those sneakers are really old.
(Let me think. / Uh-huh.)

Roberto And what else? _____ What else do I need to get?
(Oh, really? / Uh, let's see.)

Mother Well, there's one more thing you need to get . . .

Roberto What's that?

Mother A job! You need to pay for these things!

Lesson D Shop till you drop!

1 Online shopping

Reading **A** **Read the article. Who likes to shop online? Who doesn't like to shop online? Check (✓) the correct boxes.**

	Likes to shop online	Doesn't like to shop online
Sarah	☐	☐
Matt	☐	☐
Kevin	☐	☐
Susana	☐	☐

Do you like to shop online?

These days *everything* is for sale online – from movie tickets and food, to cars and houses. More and more people download music, movies, magazines, and books. It's easy and convenient. But not *everyone* likes to shop online.

Sarah Cho

"I never shop on the Internet because I like to pay cash. I don't have a credit card, and I don't want to get one. Also, I don't like to spend a lot of time online. I guess I'm not a big fan of shopping."

Matt Carson

"I work long hours – from 9:00 in the morning to 9:00 or 10:00 at night. A lot of stores close at 9:00. But the Internet never closes. I mean, I often shop at 1:00 in the morning. And the prices online are usually really cheap."

Kevin Parker

"There isn't a shopping center near my house. I have to drive an hour to the mall. Online shopping is very convenient. I buy movies, books, clothes, and food online. I never need to go out to a store."

Susana Rivera

"I like to shop with friends. We get up early and go to the mall together. We have a great time. We have lunch and look at the clothes together. When you shop online, you don't spend time with friends. You're alone."

B **Read the article again. Then write *Sarah*, *Matt*, *Kevin*, or *Susana* next to the statements.**

1. "I don't like to shop online or in stores!" *Sarah*
2. "I like to shop online because I never have to leave my home." _____
3. "I like to shop online because the prices aren't expensive." _____
4. "I don't like to shop online because I like to go to the mall with friends." _____
5. "I like to shop online because I don't have time during the day." _____
6. "I don't like to shop online because I don't like to go on the Internet." _____

2 What do you think?

Writing **A** **Why do people like to shop online? Why do people hate to shop online? Check (✓) the correct box.**

I like to shop online . . .	I hate to shop online . . .	Reasons
☐	☐	because I always buy things I don't need.
☐	☐	because it's easy to compare prices.
☐	☐	because it's convenient.
☐	☐	because you don't always have to pay sales tax.
☐	☐	because I often get "spam" emails from shopping websites.

B **Answer these questions. Try to write more than *Yes* or *No*.**

1. Do you live near a mall or shopping center? _____
2. Do you have time to shop during the week? _____
3. Do you like to go online? _____
4. Do you use a credit card? _____

C **Write a short paragraph. Use your ideas from part B, and give reasons. Start like this:**
I like to shop online because . . . **or** *I don't like to shop online because . . .*

_____

_____

_____

_____

Unit 8 Progress chart

	What can you do? Mark the boxes. ✓ = I can . . . ? = I need to review how to . . .	To review, go back to these pages in the Student's Book.
Grammar	☐ use *like to, want to, need to,* and *have to* with other verbs. ☐ ask questions with *How much . . . ?* ☐ use *this, these, that,* and *those.*	76 and 77 78 and 79 79
Vocabulary	☐ name at least 12 kinds of clothes. ☐ name at least 12 accessories. ☐ name at least 8 color words.	75, 76, and 77 78 and 79 78
Conversation strategies	☐ use "time to think" expressions like *Um, . . .* and *Let's see . . . .* ☐ use *Uh-huh* and *Oh,* to show that I agree or I'm surprised.	80 81
Writing	☐ use *because* to give reasons.	83

A wide world

UNIT 9

Lesson A Sightseeing

1 Take a tour!

Vocabulary **A Complete these suggestions for tourists.**

1. In South Korea, visit *an island*.

2. In New York, take pictures from a _____.

3. In Germany, visit an old _____.

4. See a _____ of a famous writer in Paris.

5. In Rio de Janeiro, spend a day at the _____.

6. In Egypt, walk around the _____.

7. In London, see a famous _____.

8. Go up a _____ and get a good view of Tokyo.

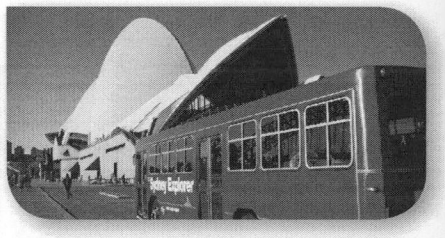

9. Take a _____ of the city in Sydney.

Grammar and vocabulary **B Can you do any of the things in part A in your city or town? Write true sentences.**

1. *In my area, you can visit an island.* **or** *In my area, you can't visit an island.*
2. _____
3. _____
4. _____
5. _____
6. _____
7. _____
8. _____
9. _____

2 What can you do in Toronto?

Grammar **A** **Read the guidebook. What can you do in Toronto? Complete the chart below.**

TORONTO, CANADA

1. The CN Tower

Get a good view of the city from 553 meters (1,814 feet). A restaurant, shops, and a glass floor!

Hours: 10:00 a.m. to 11:00 p.m.

2. Casa Loma

Toronto's only castle.
Call for a tour.

Open 9:30 a.m. to 5:00 p.m.
(Last entry at 4:00 p.m.)

3. Yorkville

Walk around a lively historic neighborhood! Outdoor cafés, shops, and movie theaters.

4. The Art Gallery of Ontario

Hours: 10:00 a.m. to 5:30 p.m.

5. Centre Island

Take the ferry to Centre Island. Enjoy beautiful parks, great restaurants, and a children's amusement park.

Open all day.

6. Harbourfront Centre

Right on Lake Ontario, this huge center has everything for all the family. Ice skating, art, cafés, a music garden, shops, sailing, and boat tours. In the summer, there are outdoor concerts, a market, and special events.

Open from 10:00 a.m. to 9:00 p.m.

On a rainy day	On a sunny day	In the evening	With children
You can go to the Art Gallery of Ontario.			

B **Complete the conversations with *can* or *can't*.**

1. **Jill** What ___*can*___ you do at Harbourfront Centre?
   Dan Let's see . . . you _____ rent a boat. And at night, you _____ go to an outdoor concert.
   Jill Sounds great! _____ we go right now?
   Dan No, we _____ . It opens at 10:00 a.m., and it's only 7:30 a.m. now. It's really early.
   Jill Oh, you're right. Well, _____ we go to a café for breakfast?
   Dan Yes, we _____ do that. Let's go!

2. **Yoshi** I'm tired today. I don't want to go on another walking tour! Where _____ we go to relax?
   Keiko Let's go to Yorkville. We _____ have a nice lunch and see a movie.
   Yoshi OK, but we _____ spend a lot of money. We need to save our money for shopping!

Lesson B Countries

1 What countries do you know?

Vocabulary **A** Complete the names of the countries. Then write the countries in the chart below.

1. S_p_ai_n_
2. ____ ____ str____ l____ ____
3. ____ or____ cc____
4. C____ st____ ____ ic____
5. R____ ss____ ____
6. M____ x____ c____
7. P____ r____
8. Fr____ nc____
9. S____ ____ th
   K____ r____ ____
10. Ch____ n____
11. Th____ ____ l____ nd
12. I____ d____ ____
13. J____ p____ n
14. C____ n____ d____
15. Br____ z____ l

I know a lot about . . .			
I don't know a lot about . . .			
They speak English in . . .			
I love the food from . . .			
I don't want to go to . . .			

B Look at the pictures. What kinds of food are these dishes? Write the nationalities.

1. *Japanese*

2. _____

3. _____

4. _____

C Complete the chart.

Food I like	Food I don't like	Food I want to try	Food I can cook
Korean			*French*

2 Where in the world?

Vocabulary **Complete the crossword puzzle.**

Across

2. There are no cities in this cold, icy region.
6. This country is in both Europe and Asia.
7. This large region includes Japan and South Korea.
9. Beijing, Shanghai, and Hong Kong are in this country.
10. This long, thin country is in South America.

Down

1. They speak both French and English in this North American country.
3. They speak this language in Turkey.
4. Rome, Venice, and Milan are cities in this European country.
5. This large country is in Oceania.
8. They speak this language in Thailand.

3 About you

Grammar **Unscramble the questions. Then write true answers.**

1. can / sports / play / What / your best friend ?
   A *What sports can your best friend play?*
   B _____

2. food / mother / make / Can / Mexican / your ?
   A _____
   B _____

3. speak / you / languages / can / What ?
   A _____
   B _____

4. your / speak / English / parents / Can ?
   A _____
   B _____

Lesson C They're a kind of candy.

1 What's this? What are these?

Conversation strategies **What are the things in the pictures? Write sentences. Use the words in the box.**

candy dress drink ✓musical instrument sandwich shoe

1. *It's a kind of musical instrument. It's called an erhu.*

2. *They're a kind of They're called*

3. _____

4. _____

5. _____

6. _____

2 What's an *Inukshuk*?

Conversation strategies **Complete the sentences. Then unscramble the letters from the boxes to find the answer to the question.**

1. A sneaker is a kind of [s] _h_ _o_ _e_.
2. A *tortilla* is kind of like a _p_ ___ ___ ___ [a] ___ ___.
3. A *balalaika* is like a _g_ ___ ___ [t] ___ ___.
4. *Gazpacho* is a kind of tomato _s_ ___ [ ] _p_.
5. *Lassi* is kind of like a ___ ___ ___ _k_ _s_ ___ ___ ___ [e].
6. Volleyball is a kind of ___ _p_ ___ _r_ [ ].

What's an *Inukshuk*?

It's like a _s_ ___ ___ _t_ ___ _e_. You can see them in Alaska and Greenland.

3 It's a kind of pot.

Conversation strategies **Complete the conversations. Use *like*, *kind of like*, or *a kind of*.**

1. A That's a beautiful dish!
   B Thanks. Actually, it's _a kind of_ pot. It's Japanese.
   A Can you cook with it? It looks so pretty.
   B Yeah! You can make Japanese food _____ *yosenabe* in it.
   A Like what?
   B Yosenabe. It's _____ soup.

2. A What can you buy at the market?
   B Well, you can buy food from different countries, things _____ fruit. You can buy durians . . .
   A What's a durian?
   B It's _____ fruit.
   A Really?
   B Yeah. It's _____ a melon.
   A Is it good?
   B Yes, I love it.

1 FAQs about Paris

Reading **A Read the website. Write the correct question heading for each paragraph.**

Where can you eat in Paris?
✓What are great places to visit in Paris?
What do people wear in Paris?
How can I travel around Paris?

http://www.parispage...

THE PARIS PAGE

Find out all you need to know about Paris! You can send your questions here for other travelers to answer. Or share your information about your trip to Paris.

Frequently Asked Questions (FAQs)

What are great places to visit in Paris?

You have to see the Eiffel Tower on your first visit. Then go to the Louvre. It's a very large and famous art museum. There are also beautiful gardens near it. After that, you can visit the Latin Quarter. It's a very old neighborhood. It has a lot of historic buildings, museums, and great shopping. More

_____

It's easy to travel in Paris. There are trains, buses, and subways. Try the subway system, called the Metro. There are 301 Metro stations in the city. Every building in Paris is near a Metro station, so it's very convenient, too! More

_____

Parisians love food. There are amazing cafés, bistros, and other kinds of restaurants everywhere in the city. You can relax at an outdoor café all day. Cafés open early in the morning and usually close late in the evening. More

_____

Parisians like to "dress up" and wear designer clothes. They don't usually wear shorts, sneakers, or T-shirts to restaurants or concerts. You can wear casual clothes and shoes in Paris, but try to look nice. More

Next

B Read the website again. Then write *T* (true) or *F* (false) for each sentence. Correct the false sentences.

1. The Louvre is a famous garden in Paris. *F* *The Louvre is a famous art museum in Paris.*
2. The Latin Quarter is a historic building. ____ _____
3. The Metro is a museum in Paris. ____ _____
4. A bistro is a kind of restaurant. ____ _____
5. Cafés open late in Paris. ____ _____
6. Parisians like to wear casual clothes when they go out. ____ _____

2 FAQs about your country

Writing **A Complete each sentence with three things about your city or country. Make lists and use commas.**

1. *El Salvador* is famous for *its beautiful beaches, outdoor markets, and great food* .
2. _____ is famous for _____ .
3. There are great places to see. You can visit _____ .
4. The people usually wear _____ .

B Imagine you are looking at a travel website about your country or city. Write answers to these questions.

TRAVEL

1. I often travel there on business, but I don't usually have a lot of time. Where can I go and what can I see in one day?

_____

_____

_____

2. I want to visit this summer, but I don't have a lot of money. What can I do for free?

_____

_____

_____

3. Where can I meet local people? What traditional things can I see or do?

_____

_____

_____

Unit 9 Progress chart

	What can you do? Mark the boxes. ✓ = I can . . . ? = I need to review how to . . .	To review, go back to these pages in the Student's Book.
Grammar	☐ use *can* and *can't* to talk about things to do in a city. ☐ use *can* and *can't* to talk about ability.	86 and 87 88 and 89
Vocabulary	☐ use at least 10 new sightseeing words. ☐ name at least 15 countries and 5 regions. ☐ name at least 10 nationalities and 10 languages.	86 and 87 88 88 and 89
Conversation strategies	☐ use *a kind of* and *kind of like* to explain new words. ☐ use *like* to give examples.	90 91
Writing	☐ use commas to separate items in a list.	93

Busy lives

UNIT 10

Lesson A A night at home

1 What did they do last night?

Grammar **What did these people do last night? What didn't they do? Complete two sentences for each picture. Use the simple past.**

1. Kate *stayed home* _____.
   She *didn't visit her parents* _____.

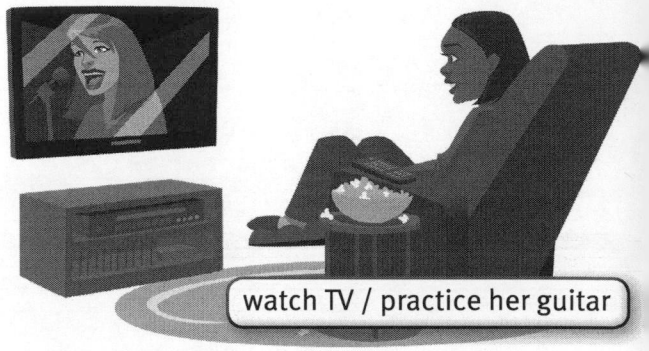

2. Rita _____.
   She _____.

3. Mee-Sun _____.
   She _____.

4. Ali and Sam _____.
   They _____.

5. Emil _____.
   He _____.

6. Joe and Ken _____.
   They _____.

2 How was your weekend?

Grammar **Complete Grace's email. Use the simple past.**

New Message

To: Paulina Lopez
From: Grace Chen
Subject: How was your weekend?

Hi Paulina!

I really *enjoyed* (enjoy) the weekend! I _____ (invite) a friend over on Saturday. She's my co-worker, and she's very nice. We _____ (play) tennis in the morning and _____ (stay) at the tennis club for lunch. Then we _____ (practice) yoga and _____ (walk) in the park.

In the evening, we _____ (watch) a movie and _____ (cook) a big dinner. We _____ (talk) a lot, but we _____ (not talk) about work. And we _____ (not watch) TV all day – a nice change!

Then on Sunday, I _____ (study) English and _____ (clean) the house. Hey! You _____ (not call) me on Sunday! Call me soon, OK? Tell me about your weekend.

Grace

3 About you

Grammar and vocabulary **Write true sentences about your weekend. Use the simple past. Add more information.**

1. invite a friend over *I invited a friend over for dinner.* **or** *I didn't invite a friend over for dinner.*
2. stay home _____
3. study for an exam _____
4. clean the house _____
5. call a friend _____
6. check my email _____
7. chat online _____
8. practice my English _____
9. listen to music _____
10. rent a car _____
11. cook a big meal _____
12. exercise _____

Lesson B A busy week

1 A weekly planner

Grammar and vocabulary **Read Jenna's planner. Then complete the sentences below. Use the simple past of the verbs in the box.**

SUNDAY	MONDAY	TUESDAY	WEDNESDAY
Movie with Meg 1:00 ✓ *Romeo and Juliet – Grand Theater 2:00 ✗* *Homework ✗*	*Read The Pearl ✓* *Read art magazine ✗* *Homework ✓*	*Write book report on The Pearl ✓* *Write history paper ✗* *Homework ✓*	*Piano lesson 4:30 ✗* *Doctor's appointment 2:00 ✓* *Homework ✓*
THURSDAY	**FRIDAY**	**SATURDAY**	
Call: Mom ✓ *Felipe ✓* *Lia ✓* *Make dinner 6:30 ✗* *Homework ✓*	*Alison's party 7:30 ✓* *Mike 8:00 ✗* *Homework ✓*	*Shopping! Need new:* *shoes ✗* *jacket ✓* *Homework ✗*	

buy do go have make read ✓see write

1. On Sunday, Jenna ___*saw*___ a movie.
   She ___*didn't see*___ a play.
2. On Monday, Jenna _____ a book in English.
   She _____ a magazine.
3. Jenna _____ a book report on Tuesday.
   She _____ a history paper.
4. Jenna _____ a doctor's appointment on Wednesday.
   She _____ a piano lesson this week.
5. On Thursday, Jenna _____ a lot of phone calls.
   She _____ dinner.
6. On Friday, Jenna _____ to a party.
   She _____ out with Mike.
7. Jenna _____ a new jacket on Saturday.
   She _____ new shoes.
8. Jenna _____ homework every school day.
   She _____ homework on the weekend.

2 About you

Grammar and vocabulary

A Complete the questions in the questionnaire. Use the simple past of the verbs in the box. Then write true answers. Write more than *yes* or *no*.

do eat ✓go have make see speak take write

QUESTIONNAIRE: Did you . . . ?

1. *Did* you *go* out a lot last week?
Yes, I did. I went out every night last week. **or** *No, I didn't. I stayed home.*

2. _____ you and your family _____ dinner in front of the TV last night?
_____

3. _____ you _____ anything interesting last weekend?
_____

4. _____ you _____ in a restaurant on Friday night?
_____

5. _____ your class _____ a test or an exam last week?
_____

6. _____ you _____ dinner every night last week?
_____

7. _____ your best friend _____ you an email yesterday?
_____

8. _____ your parents _____ a movie on Saturday night?
_____

9. _____ you _____ to a lot of friends in class yesterday?
_____

B Write a sentence about each day last week. Write one thing you did each day.

1. Monday _____
2. Tuesday _____
3. Wednesday _____
4. Thursday _____
5. Friday _____
6. Saturday _____
7. Sunday _____

Lesson C Congratulations!

1 Responding to news

Conversation strategies

A Complete the conversations. Circle and write the best response.

1. A I bought a new TV today.
   B *Good for you!*
   a. Good for you!
   b. I'm sorry to hear that.
   c. Good luck!

2. A I'm 25 today!
   B _____
   a. I'm sorry to hear that.
   b. Good luck!
   c. Happy birthday!

3. A My wife had a baby girl last night.
   B _____
   a. Good for you!
   b. Happy birthday!
   c. Congratulations!

4. A I have a job interview today.
   B _____
   a. I'm sorry to hear that.
   b. Good luck!
   c. Happy birthday!

5. A I finally passed my English exam.
   B _____
   a. Thank goodness!
   b. I'm sorry to hear that.
   c. Good luck!

6. A I didn't get the job I wanted.
   B _____
   a. I'm sorry to hear that.
   b. Thank goodness!
   c. Good for you!

B Your friend tells you some news, and you respond. Write the conversations.

1. Your friend bought a new car, and he got a bargain.

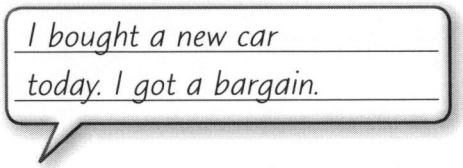

2. Your friend got 100% on her English exam.

3. Your friend finally got a job.

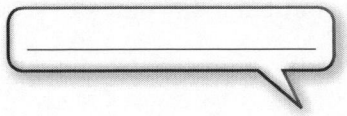

4. Your friend wanted to go on vacation, but he has no money.

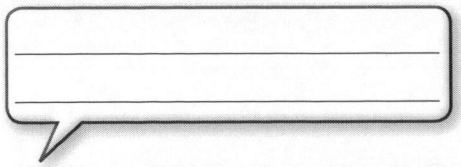

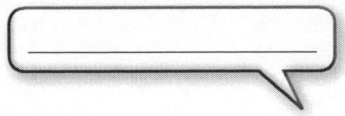

2 You did?

Conversation strategies

A Complete the conversations with the expressions in the box.

✓You did?	You did?	You did?	Good luck!	I'm sorry to hear that.	Good for you.

1. Lilly Did you have a busy day?
   Beth Yeah, I'm exhausted. I went shopping downtown.
   Lilly *You did?* Did you buy anything?
   Beth Yes, I bought a new suit. And a blouse and shoes.
   Lilly _____ _____ _____
   Beth And then I had lunch with Maria, and we talked all afternoon. How about you?
   Lilly I cleaned the house, did the laundry, and made dinner.
   Beth _____ _____ That's great! I'm starving! Let's eat!

2. Jun Did you have a good week?
   José Actually, no. I had five exams.
   Jun _____ _____ That's awful. Did you pass?
   José Well, I passed three and failed two.
   Jun Oh. _____ _____ _____ _____ _____
   José And I have two exams tomorrow, too.
   Jun _____ _____ Study hard!

B Write two responses for each piece of news.

1. I had a terrible vacation in Hawaii.

   You did? I'm sorry to hear that.

2. I took my driver's test yesterday.

   _____ _____

3. I wrote an article for a magazine last month.

   _____ _____

4. My friend and I worked all weekend.

   _____ _____

Lesson D A blog

1 A busy birthday . . .

Reading **A** **Look at the four pictures. Then read Peter's blog. Number the pictures in order from 1 to 4.**

Friday, May 28 11:45 p.m.

I had a crazy day today. I had an English exam, and it's my birthday!

I had the exam at 8:30 this morning. I needed to study, so I woke up early – at 6:30 a.m. I took a shower, made some coffee, and studied for about an hour. Well, the coffee didn't work. I fell asleep!
I woke up at 8:20 with my head on my books. I had ten minutes before the test started!

I ran outside, got on my bike, and went to English class. I got there right at 8:30, but guess what! The teacher never came! My classmates and I waited about half an hour. Then we left. It's great. Now I can really study for the exam.

I had breakfast, and then I went to my next class – math. ☹ I think math is really hard, but I have to take it. My teacher talked for an hour. I wanted to write some notes, but I fell asleep. I need to borrow my friend's notes.

After I finished class, I met my friend Louisa, and we went to a movie together. It was my birthday, so she paid! Great! We saw a new romantic drama. You know, I usually like drama movies a lot, but I didn't like that movie very much.

When I got home from the movie, my mother called and sang "Happy Birthday" to me. Now I have to stay up and finish a paper for a class tomorrow. I hope I don't fall asleep again!

Posted by Peter Miller

0 comments

B **Read the blog again. Then answer the questions. Give reasons for the answers.**

1. Did Peter get up late? *No, he didn't. He needed to study.*
2. Did Peter take an English exam? _____
3. Did he listen to his math teacher? _____
4. Did he go out with a friend? _____
5. Did Peter's mother call? _____
6. Do you think he's a good student? _____

2 My last birthday

Writing **A Read the blog on page 80 again. Match the two parts of each sentence.**

1. Peter studied when __c__
2. Peter had breakfast after ____
3. When Peter went to his math class, ____
4. Peter finished classes. Then ____
5. Peter saw a movie before ____

a. he went home.
b. he fell asleep again.
✓c. he got up in the morning.
d. he met his friend Louisa.
e. he left his English class.

B Think about a day you remember well. Answer these questions. Write more than *yes* or *no*.

1. Did you work or have classes? _____
2. Did you go out with friends? _____
3. Did you do something fun? _____
4. Did you eat any of your favorite foods? _____
5. Did you go to any stores? _____
6. Did you get home late? _____

C Write a paragraph for your own blog. Use your ideas from part B. Use *before*, *after*, *when*, or *then*, if possible.

I remember my last birthday. I _____

_____

_____

_____

_____

Unit 10 Progress chart

	What can you do? Mark the boxes. ✓ = I can . . . ? = I need to review how to . . .	To review, go back to these pages in the Student's Book.
Grammar	☐ make simple past statements with regular verbs. ☐ make simple past statements with irregular verbs. ☐ ask simple past *yes-no* questions.	98 and 99 100 and 101 101
Vocabulary	☐ make simple past forms of at least 12 regular verbs. ☐ make simple past forms of at least 8 irregular verbs. ☐ use time expressions with the simple past.	98 and 99 100 and 101 101
Conversation strategies	☐ use responses like *Good for you!* and *Congratulations!* ☐ use *You did?* to show I'm listening, surprised, or interested.	102 and 103 103
Writing	☐ use *before*, *after*, *when*, and *then* to order events.	105

Looking back

UNIT 11

Lesson A My first . . .

1 Yesterday

Vocabulary **Complete the sentences. Use the words in the box.**

busy ✓happy nervous nice quiet scared

1. Yesterday was my birthday. My friends had a party for me, and I got a lot of presents. I was very *happy* .
2. My family and I live in a very small town. There are no clubs or movie theaters. My town is really _____ – especially at night.
3. I started a new job yesterday. I was really _____ of my new boss.
4. I had a lot of things to do yesterday. I was pretty _____ .
5. My best friend's parents are friendly. They're very _____ .
6. We had a French test last week. I was really _____ , but I passed.

2 It was fun!

Vocabulary **Choose the best two words to complete each sentence. Cross out the wrong word.**

I remember my first driving lesson. Before I met the teacher, I was really ~~**scary**~~ / **nervous** / **scared**. But then I relaxed because he was very **nice** / **strict** / **friendly**. The lesson was **awful** / **good** / **fun** because I didn't make a lot of mistakes. I was pretty good. At the end of the lesson, I was **exhausted** / **lazy** / **tired**. It was hard work! After ten lessons, I took my test, but I didn't pass. I wasn't **awful** / **pleased** / **happy**. But I passed three weeks later. Now I can drive my dad's **nice** / **new** / **awful** car.

3 I remember . . .

Grammar **Complete the conversations with *was, wasn't, were,* or *weren't.***

1. **Sally** Do you remember your first date, Grandpa?
Grandpa Yes. I ___was___ 16, and the girl _____ in my class. We _____ classmates. We went to the movies.
Sally _____ you nervous?
Grandpa No, I _____ . It _____ a lot of fun.
Sally Do you remember her name?
Grandpa Yes. Grandma!

2. **Paula** I remember my first day of high school. It _____ a hot day, and I went with two of my friends.
Kenton _____ you scared?
Paula No, we _____ really scared, but I guess we _____ a little nervous.
Kenton _____ the teachers friendly?
Paula Yes, they _____ very nice. Thank goodness.

3. **Sun-Hee** Do you remember your first college English class?
Carla Yes, it _____ last year. I _____ very good at English, and I made a lot of mistakes. My partner's English _____ very good, so he _____ very happy with me!
Sun-Hee _____ he smart? I mean, intelligent?
Carla Yes, he _____ .
Sun-Hee So, was your first class fun?
Carla No, it _____ . In fact, it _____ awful.

Lesson B Vacations

1 About you

Grammar and vocabulary **A Unscramble the questions. Then write true answers.**

1. trip or vacation / was / last / your / When ?

   A *When was your last trip or vacation?*

   B _____

2. go / did / Where / exactly / you ?

   A _____

   B _____

3. weather / like / was / the / What ?

   A _____

   B _____

4. you / there / do / did / What ?

   A _____

   B _____

5. were / there / How / you / long ?

   A _____

   B _____

Grammar **B Read about Emi's first trip to the park with a friend. Write questions for the answers.**

"We weren't very old – I think I was eight, and my friend was ten. We went to the park, but my mother didn't know. We had a great time! We went swimming in the pool. I remember it was a beautiful day – warm and sunny. We were there about an hour. Then we got hungry, so we went home. When we got back, my mother wasn't too happy."

1. A *How old was Emi?*

   B Eight.

2. A _____

   B To the park.

3. A _____

   B Her friend.

4. A _____

   B They went swimming.

5. A _____

   B Warm and sunny.

6. A _____

   B About an hour.

2 *Get* and *go*

Vocabulary **A** **Which of these expressions do you use with *get*? Which do you use with *go*? Which can you use with *get* and *go*? Complete the chart.**

✓back	to bed	scared	swimming	to the movies	a view of something
✓lost	a gift	skiing	(an) autograph	snorkeling	along with someone
home	hiking	camping	on vacation	a bad sunburn	to see a concert / movie
sick	biking	married	up early or late	on a road trip	to the beach

get	*go*	*get* and *go*
lost		*back*

B **Complete the questions with *get* or *go*. Then write your own answers.**

1. A What time do you ___*go* **or** *get*___ to bed on weeknights?
   B _____

2. A How often do you _____ swimming?
   B _____

3. A Did you _____ a bad sunburn last year?
   B _____

4. A What did you _____ for your last birthday?
   B _____

5. A Can you think of someone you don't _____ along with?
   B _____

6. A Where do you want to _____ on vacation this year?
   B _____

7. A Do you _____ up early in the morning?
   B _____

Lesson C Anyway, what did *you* do?

1 Asking questions

Conversation strategies **Complete each conversation with two questions.**

1. **Sadie** How was your weekend?
   Bill It was awful. We went hang gliding. I hated it!
   Sadie That's too bad.
   Bill Yeah. Anyway, how about you?
   What did you do?
   Did you do anything special?
   Sadie Well, we rented a car and went camping.
   Bill That sounds nice.

2. **Dirk** Did you go out last night?
   Leo Yeah, I met a friend and went to a club.
   _____
   _____
   Dirk Oh, I went to the laundromat and did my laundry. I didn't do anything exciting.

3. **Shira** I went to the concert last Saturday.
   Jaz I did, too! The band sounded great.
   _____
   _____
   Shira Oh, it was fantastic. Well, anyway, it's 11:30.
   Jaz Yeah, it's late. See you tomorrow.

4. **Gabor** So, did you work last weekend?
   Koji Yeah, Saturday and Sunday. We were really busy.
   _____
   _____
   Gabor Let's see . . . I went shopping, um, and saw a movie. Then on Sunday, I played tennis, made dinner, . . .
   Koji I guess you were busy, too!

2 Well, anyway, . . .

Conversation strategies

A Use *anyway* three times in this conversation. Leave two of the blanks empty.

Mirka Where were you last week? Were you away?

Arlen Yes, I was in Mexico on business.

Mirka Mexico? What was that like?

Arlen Oh, great. The customers there are really nice. _____ I always enjoy my trips to Mexico. The people are so friendly.

Mirka That's nice. _____ So you're traveling a lot these days.

Arlen Yeah. About six times a year. _____, what about you? Did you have a good week?

Mirka Not bad. I had a lot of meetings – you know, the usual. _____, do you want to go out tonight? We can have dinner maybe.

Arlen Sure. We can meet after work.

Mirka OK. Well, _____, I have to go. See you later.

B Use the instructions to complete the conversations.

1. **Friend** What do you usually do on the weekends?

   You *I usually go out with friends. What about you?*
   (Answer. Then ask a question about your friend.)

   Friend Me? I usually go to see a movie. Sometimes a friend and I go camping or hiking.

2. **Friend** I'm enjoying my new job. My boss is OK, and the people are nice. We get along – it's a friendly place.

   You That's nice. _____
   (Change the topic. Invite your friend for dinner tomorrow.)

   Friend Tomorrow? Sounds great. What time? Seven?

3. **Friend** What did you do for your last birthday?

   You _____
   (Answer. Then end the conversation. It's late.)

   Friend OK. Talk to you later.

4. **Friend** So how was your weekend?

   You _____
   (Answer. Then change the topic. Invite your friend to do something fun next weekend.)

   Friend Sure. Sounds like fun.

1 My first job

Reading **A** **Read the story. What are these people like? Match the names with the adjectives.**

1. Diana *a*
2. Joe _____
3. Megan _____
4. Rick _____

✓a. friendly
b. nervous
c. good looking
d. strict

Tell Us About Your First Job

Reader Megan Walker writes in with a story about her first job.

I remember my first job. I worked in an outdoor café one summer. It was called Sunny's. I got free drinks and food. My boss Diana was very friendly, and I got along well with her. Her husband Joe worked there, too, but he was really strict. On my first day, I was late because I got lost on the subway. After that, Joe was never too happy with me.

So, every day I served sandwiches and coffee. The café was really busy all the time. I wasn't a very good server, so I was often nervous. Also, I was always exhausted by the end of the day.

One day, I was really tired, so I asked to go home early. Joe looked angry, but he said, "OK. Fine." I left and went to the subway. Then I met my friend Rick on the street. He was really good looking, and I liked him a lot. He said, "Do you want to go and eat something?" I said, "Yes. OK. Where?" And he said, "I know a café near here. Let's go there. They have good sandwiches."

So we went back to Sunny's and sat down to eat! We waited for about ten minutes before Joe finally came over to the table. He was very busy, so he didn't look at me. He said, "I'm sorry. One of the servers left early. Are you ready to order?" We stayed for an hour. I was lucky because my boss never saw me, but I had to pay for my sandwich and soda!

– Megan Walker
New York City

B **Read Megan's story again. Then answer the questions.**

1. Where did Megan work? *She worked at Sunny's.*
2. How did Megan get to work? _____
3. What kind of food did she serve? _____
4. What was the café like? _____
5. Why did she leave early one day? _____
6. Why did she go back to Sunny's? _____
7. How long did they stay at Sunny's? _____

2 He said, . . .

Writing **A Read the rest of the story. Rewrite their conversation after they leave the café. Use quoted speech. Add capital letters and correct punctuation (" " , . ?).**

Rick and I left the café and talked for a few minutes.

rick asked how did you like the café *Rick asked, "How did you like the café?"*

I said it's nice _____

he said the service wasn't very good _____

I said well one of the servers left early _____

rick said people are so lazy these days _____

I said yes I know _____

But I didn't tell Rick I was the server!

B Think about a time you met a friend for the first time. Answer these questions.

1. How old were you? _____
2. What was your friend's name? _____
3. How did you first meet? What happened? _____
4. What did you say when you first met? I said, "_____."
5. What did your friend say? She / He said, "_____."

C Now write a story about meeting your friend. Use your ideas from part B.

When we met, I was 13 and _____ . _____

_____

_____

_____

Unit 11 Progress chart

What can you do? Mark the boxes. ✓ = I can . . . ? = I need to review how to . . .	To review, go back to these pages in the Student's Book.
Grammar	
☐ make simple past statements and questions with *be*.	108 and 109
☐ ask simple past information questions.	110
Vocabulary	
☐ name at least 12 words to describe people or experiences.	108 and 109
☐ name at least 4 new expressions with *go*.	111
☐ name at least 5 new expressions with *get*.	111
Conversation strategies	
☐ ask and answer questions to show interest.	112
☐ use *Anyway* to change the topic or end a conversation.	113
Writing	
☐ use capitals and punctuation in quoted speech.	115

Fabulous food

UNIT 12

Lesson A Eating habits

1 Mmmmm!

Vocabulary **Write the names of the foods. Then find the words in the puzzle. Look in these directions (→ ↓).**

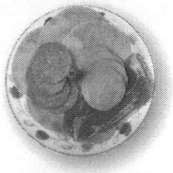

1. *meat*

2. *seafood*

3. _____

4. _____

5. _____

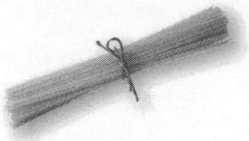

6. _____

7. _____

F	F	V	C	A	R	R	O	T	S
R	X	E	B	I	B	E	E	F	S
U	O	G	A	X	R	M	E	A	T
I	A	E	N	S	E	I	S	T	A
T	E	T	A	E	A	L	L	C	E
G	G	A	N	A	D	K	F	H	P
P	G	B	A	F	R	U	I	E	P
O	S	L	S	O	P	P	D	E	A
T	F	E	N	O	U	D	L	S	S
A	I	S	Z	D	I	H	G	E	T
T	S	H	R	I	C	E	F	Q	A
O	H	C	H	I	C	K	E	N	M
E	C	U	C	U	M	B	E	R	S
S	H	E	L	L	F	I	S	H	Z

8. _____

9. _____

10. _____

11. _____

12. _____

13. _____

14. _____

15. _____

16. _____

17. _____

18. _____

2 An invitation to dinner

Grammar **A** **Read the invitation. Then circle the correct words to complete the emails.**

New Message

Hi Jenny,
Thanks for the invitation. A question for you – how **much / many** friends can I bring? Can I bring three? Oh, and I don't eat **beef / beefs**. I'm not 100% vegetarian because I eat **chicken / chickens** and I like **fish / fishes**. I'm allergic to **milk / milks**, and I don't eat **a lot of / much** eggs, either.
See you on Saturday!
Pam

New Message

Dear Jenny,
Thanks for the invitation. See you Saturday.
Did I tell you? I'm on a diet this week, so I'm not eating **much / many** cheese or pasta – I'm just eating **many / a lot of** fruit and vegetables.
I mean, how **many / much** fruit can a guy eat?
Bye.
Dave

B **Write your own email to Jenny. Tell her about these foods.**

- food you like
- food you don't like
- food you eat a lot of
- food you don't eat a lot of

New Message

Dear Jenny,
Thanks for the invitation to the party. _____

_____
_____
_____
_____
_____

3 About you

Grammar and vocabulary **Complete the questions with *How much* or *How many*. Then write your own answers.**

1. *How many* students in your class are vegetarians? _____
2. _____ milk does your family buy every week? _____
3. _____ times a week do you eat chicken? _____
4. _____ shellfish do you eat? Do you eat a lot? _____
5. _____ of your friends are picky eaters? _____
6. _____ cans of soda do you drink a day? _____

1 At the supermarket

Vocabulary **Write the words under the pictures. Then write the food in the chart below.**

1. *apples* 2. _____ 3. _____ 4. _____ 5. _____

6. _____ 7. _____ 8. _____ 9. _____ 10. _____

11. _____ 12. _____ 13. _____ 14. _____ 15. _____

16. _____ 17. _____ 18. _____ 19. _____ 20. _____

meat and seafood	fruit	vegetables	other
	apples		

2 What would you like?

Grammar **Complete the conversations. Use *would you like* or *'d like*.**

1. Jim What *would you like* ?
   Megan I _____ ice cream, please.
   Jim _____ chocolate sprinkles?
   Megan Yes, please.

2. Server Good evening. _____ something to drink?
   Dan Oh, just water, please.
   Server OK. And what _____ to eat?
   Dan Um, I _____ the salmon, please.
   Server _____ some green beans with it?
   Dan Actually, I _____ some spinach, please.

3. Greg Where _____ to go for dinner?
   Sheila Oh, I don't know. I _____ to go somewhere around here.
   Greg _____ to try the new Thai restaurant?
   Sheila Oh, yes! I _____ something spicy.

3 *Some* or *any*

Grammar **Complete the conversations with *some* or *any*.**

1. Ming Polly, try *some* lamb.
   Polly Gosh, it's hot! I need _____ water . . . now!
   Ming Here. Drink _____ soda.

2. John Do you have _____ chocolate cookies?
   Ken No, but we have _____ peanut butter cookies.
   John OK, I'll take _____ .

3. Sara Would you like _____ potato chips?
   Craig Yeah, but I don't have _____ money.
   Sara Oh, and I don't have _____ , either.

Lesson C A sandwich or something

1 Something for lunch

Conversation strategies **Complete the conversation with *or something* or *or anything*.**

Trish Do you go out for lunch every day or . . . ?

Pete Well, I don't usually eat lunch. I don't like to eat a big meal *or anything* at lunchtime.

Trish No? You don't have a snack _____ ?

Pete Well, I sometimes have a hot drink, like hot chocolate _____ .

Trish Well, I'm hungry – I'd like a sandwich _____ . Would you like something to eat?

Pete Well, maybe . . .

Trish How about a salad _____ ?

Pete Yes, OK. Actually, I'd like a chicken sandwich. Oh, let's get some ice cream _____ , too. I guess I *am* hungry!

2 About you

Conversation strategies **Answer the questions. Write true answers. Use *or something* or *or anything*.**

1. Are you a picky eater? *Well, I don't eat fish or shrimp or anything.*
2. What do you usually have for dinner? _____
3. How about lunch? _____
4. What do you like to order in restaurants? _____
5. What do you drink with meals? _____
6. What kinds of snacks do you like? _____

3 Would you like to go out or . . . ?

Conversation strategies

Complete the conversations. Which questions can end with *or* . . . ? Add *or* . . . where possible.

1. **Paul** What would you like for dinner tonight _____ ?
   Would you like to go out *or . . .* ?
   Val Yes, please! I'd love to eat out.
   Paul That's great. So can I choose the restaurant _____ ?
   Val Sure.
   Paul Let's see . . . would you like a pizza _____ ?
   Val Um, I don't want Italian tonight. How about an Asian place? Do you like Korean or Thai _____ ?
   Paul Uh, I don't really care for spicy food.
   Val Let me think . . . do you want to get a hamburger _____ ?
   Paul Yeah! With maybe some French fries and some cookies.
   Val OK! Stop! I'm starving! Let's go!

2. **Kate** It's my birthday today.
   Sally Happy birthday! Do you have plans _____ ?
   Kate I had plans, but my friend just called. He's sick.
   Sally That's terrible! I know. Let's eat at my house. I can cook some steaks or something. What do you think _____ ?
   Kate That's very nice, thanks, but I'm a vegetarian.
   Sally Oh. Do you eat pasta _____ ?
   Kate Well, I can't eat pasta or anything heavy right now. I'm on a diet.
   Sally OK. No pasta. What would you like _____ ?
   Kate Do you have any fruit _____ ?
   Sally Sorry. I ate the last banana this morning before I went to work. I have some carrots. . . .
   Kate Let's stop at the supermarket on our way to your house.

1 Healthy fast food

Reading **A Read the blog post. Find the answers to these questions.**

1. Where did the writer eat breakfast? _____
2. What breakfast food does the writer recommend? _____
3. How many calories were in the writer's lunch? _____

TASTES GOOD, AND GOOD FOR YOU!

We often think of fast food as hamburgers, fried chicken, hot dogs, and French fries. However, some fast-food restaurants are starting to offer healthy foods, too. But how healthy is "healthy" fast-food, and how does it taste? I went to some famous fast-food restaurants last week to find the answer and was pleasantly surprised. Here are the two healthy fast-food choices I recommend.

BURGER RESTAURANTS: OATMEAL, PLEASE!

Many burger restaurants open early and serve breakfast, too. One popular restaurant chain has a breakfast with more than 1,000 calories. That's about half the calories you need for a whole day! For a healthy option, you can now choose apple slices (15 calories), fruit and nuts (210 calories), or oatmeal (290 calories). I tried the oatmeal, and it was delicious!

MEXICAN RESTAURANTS: I'D LIKE IT IN A BOWL

I love Mexican fast food as a special treat, but I'm pleased to see that my favorite taco restaurant now has a lot of healthy choices on the menu. A taco salad with beef and cheese is about 600 calories. However, I went for chicken. You can make your own meal with chicken, rice, tomatoes, and other healthy foods. I tried it for lunch. I got it in a bowl and said no to the tortilla chips. It was very tasty and only 450 calories.

Do you know any great, healthy fast-food places? Tell us in the comments section.

B Read the blog post again. Then choose the correct words to complete these sentences.

1. The writer wanted to try some **hamburgers / healthy food** last week.
2. He thinks that 1,000 calories **is / is not** a lot for breakfast.
3. He **enjoyed / didn't enjoy** the oatmeal.
4. He had **taco salad / chicken** for lunch.
5. He **ate / didn't eat** tortilla chips with his lunch.
6. His lunch was **very / not very** healthy.

2 Restaurant reviews

Writing **A Jill Heacock is a restaurant reviewer. She ate at the Seafood Palace last week, and she loved it. Circle the correct words to complete Jill's review.**

THIS WEEK'S RESTAURANT: **THE SEAFOOD PALACE** ★ ★ ★ ★

by Jill Heacock

Last week, I went to the Seafood Palace – it's a **terrible / wonderful** restaurant. I loved it. I was there on a busy night, and the atmosphere was **fun / formal**. The food was **awful / delicious**, and every dish came to the table **cold / hot**. I really liked the shrimp. Very tasty! The service was **excellent / slow**, the servers were really **friendly / lazy**, and the meal was **cheap / expensive**. I only spent $12!

The Seafood Palace is a good place to hang out with friends or have dinner with your family. Try it!

B Imagine you are a restaurant reviewer. You ate at a restaurant, and you hated it. Write your review.

THIS WEEK'S RESTAURANT: _____ ★

by _____

Last week, I went to _____ – it's a terrible restaurant! _____

_____

_____

_____

_____

_____

Unit 12 Progress chart

What can you do? Mark the boxes. ✓ = I can . . . ? = I need to review how to . . .	To review, go back to these pages in the Student's Book.
Grammar	
☐ use countable and uncountable nouns.	118 and 119
☐ make statements and questions with *much, many,* and *a lot of.*	118 and 119
☐ make statements and questions with *some, any,* and *not any.*	120 and 121
☐ make offers and requests with *would like.*	121
Vocabulary	
☐ name at least 5 categories of food.	118 and 119
☐ name at least 25 different foods.	118, 119, and 120
Conversation strategies	
☐ use *or something* and *or anything.*	122
☐ use *or . . . ?* in *yes-no* questions to make them less direct.	123
Writing	
☐ use expressions to talk about restaurants.	124 and 125

Illustration credits

Ken Batelman: 42 **Harry Briggs:** 15, 61 *(4 at bottom)*, 69 **Domninic Bugatto:** 8, 23, 27, 38, 59, 78 **Cambridge University Press:** 67 **Matt Collins:** 22, 54 **Chuck Gonzales:** 5, 11, 26, 45, 80 **Cheryl Hoffman:** 3, 24, 47, 61 *(2 at top)* **Jon Keegan:** 19, 51, 94, 95 **Frank Montagna:** 2, 13, 21, 53, 82, 83 **Greg White:** 7, 16, 37, 79 **Terry Wong:** 30, 46, 63, 74, 86 **Filip Yip:** 70

Photo credits

3 *(clockwise from top left)* ©Exactostock/SuperStock; ©Elea Dumas/Getty Images; ©MIXA/Getty Images; ©Thinkstock **4** ©Ryan McVay/Getty Images **7** ©wavebreakmedia/Shutterstock **10** *(clockwise from top left)* ©Andresr/Shutterstock; ©MTPA Stock/Masterfile; ©Spencer Grant/PhotoEdit; ©Jose Luiz Pelaez Inc./Corbis; ©Medioimages/Photodisc/Thinkstock; ©Terry Doyle/Getty Images **11** *(top to bottom)* ©Image Source/SuperStock; ©kurhan/Shutterstock **12** *(pen)* ©Phant/Shutterstock; *(potato chips)* ©Thinkstock; *(wallet)* ©AlexTois/Shutterstock; *(laptop)* ©Alex Staroseltsev/Shutterstock; *(umbrella)* ©K. Miri Photography/Shutterstock; *(bag)* ©Hemera Technologies/Thinkstock; *(glasses)* ©Ingvar Bjork/Shutterstock; *(keys)* ©SELEZNEV VALERY/Shutterstock; *(notebook)* ©zirconicusso/Shutterstock; *(smartphone)* ©Oleksiy Mark/Shutterstock; *(water bottle)* ©lucadp/Shutterstock; *(eraser)* ©GreenStockCreative/Shutterstock; *(watch)* ©Venus Angel/Shutterstock; ©Butterfly Hunter/Shutterstock; *(pencil)* ©Julia Ivantsova/Shutterstock; *(hand holding smartphone)* ©Thinkstock; *(hand holding water bottle)* ©DenisNata/Shutterstock; *(all others)* ©George Kerrigan **14** *(top row, left to right)* ©Rtimages/Shutterstock; ©Cambridge University Press; ©Thinkstock; ©Cambridge University Press *(middle row, left to right)* ©Ryan McVay/Thinkstock; ©Ryan McVay/Thinkstock; ©Thinkstock; ©Pixtal/age Fotostock *(bottom row, left to right)* ©Cambridge University Press; ©Cambridge University Press; ©Photodisc/Thinkstock; ©vovan/Shutterstock **19** ©Design Pics/SuperStock **20** *(clockwise from top left)* ©Exactostock/SuperStock; ©Exactostock/SuperStock; ©Mark Scott/Getty Images; ©Fancy Collection/SuperStock; ©Andreas Pollok/Getty Images; ©Ron Chapple/Getty Images; ©rSnapshotPhotos/Shutterstock; ©Peter Cade/Getty Images **28** ©Don Nichols/Getty Images **29** *(top to bottom)* ©Larry Dale Gordon/Getty Image; ©Punchstock **32** *(television)* ©Maxx-Studio/Shutterstock **35** *(top to bottom)* ©Darren Mower/Getty Images; ©Thinkstock **36** *(top row, left to right)* ©JOSE LUIS SALMERON Notimex/Newscom; ©The Everett Collection; ©The Everett Collection; ©Getty Images *(bottom row, left to right)* ©Lions Gate/courtesy Everett Collection; ©Eric Roberts/Corbis; ©Robert Voets/CBS via Getty Images; ©Ann Johansson/Corbis **40** ©violetblue/Shutterstock **43** *(left to right)* ©Maxx-Studio/Shutterstock; ©MariusdeGraf/Shutterstock **44** *(clockwise from top left)* ©Cambridge University Press; ©Artur Synenko/Shutterstock; ©Cambridge University Press; ©Cambridge University Press; ©Cambridge University Press; ©Cambridge University Press **45** ©Punchstock **47** ©Anders Blomqvist/Getty Images **48** *(left to right)* ©Ambient Images Inc./Alamy; ©Yellow Dog Productions/Getty Images; ©Spencer Grant/PhotoEdit; ©David Grossman/Imageworks **50** *(clockwise from top left)* ©Holly Harris/Getty Images; © Kwame Zikomo/SuperStock; © Jens Lucking/Getty Image; © Kaz Chiba/Getty Images; © Onoky/SuperStock; © I. Hatz/Masterfile **52** *(top row, all photos)* ©Cambridge University Press *(middle row, left to right)* ©Cambridge University Press; ©Rudy Umans/Shutterstock; ©JupiterImages *(bottom row, left to right)* ©JupiterImages; ©Cambridge University Press; ©Danilo Calilung/Corbis **56** ©Mike Powell/Getty Images **58** *(sweater)* ©Karina Bakalyan/Shutterstock; *(skirt)* ©Ruslan Kudrin/Shutterstock; *(jeans)* ©Karkas/Shutterstock *(all others)* ©Cambridge University Press **60** ©George Kerrigan **64** *(clockwise from top left)* ©Belinda Images/SuperStock; ©Ingram Publishing/SuperStock; ©Blend Images/SuperStock; ©Punchstock *(mouse)* ©urfin/Shutterstock **66** *(top row, left to right)* ©Catherine Karnow/Corbis; ©Shawn Baldwin/EPA/Newscom; ©Fotosonline/Alamy *(middle row, left to right)* ©Peter Willi/SuperStock; ©Douglas Pulsipher/Alamy; ©KSTFoto/Alamy (bottom row, left to right) ©Cambridge University Press; ©Prisma Bildagentur AG/Alamy; ©S.T. Yiap Still Life/Alamy **67** (top to bottom) ©Bob Krist/Corbis; ©Ron Erwin/Getty Images; ©Bert Hoferichter/Alamy **68** *(clockwise from top left)* ©Enzo/agefotostock; ©Olga Lyubkina/Shutterstock; ©Olga Miltsova/Shutterstock; ©Joseph Dilag/Shutterstock **69** ©Steve Hix/Somos Images/Corbis **71** *(top to bottom)* ©Laura Coles/Getty Images; ©Datacraft Co Ltd/Getty Images; ©panda3800/Shutterstock **72** *(top to bottom)* ©Stephen Johnson/Getty Images; ©Simon DesRochers/Masterfile; ©ImagesEurope/Alamy; ©David Robinson/Snap2000 Images/Alamy75 © Best View Stock/Alamy **76** ©Thinkstock **82** ©Thinkstock **84** *(top to bottom)* ©Exactostock/SuperStock; ©Joe McBride/Getty Images **85** ©David Young-Wolff/PhotoEdit **87** ©Blend Images/SuperStock **90** *(clockwise from top left)* ©Cambridge University Press; ©Alexander Raths/Shutterstock; ©Cambridge University Press; ©Africa Studio/Shutterstock; ©Cambridge University Press; ©Cambridge University Press; ©Cambridge University Press; ©Cambridge University Press; ©Cambridge University Press; ©Lepas/Shutterstock; ©Luis Carlos Jimenez del rio/Shutterstock; ©Jonelle Weaver/Getty Images; ©Cambridge University Press; ©Tetra Images/SuperStock; ©Cambridge University Press; ©Nixx Photography/Shutterstock; ©Orange Stock Photo Production Inc./Alamy; ©simpleman/Shutterstock **91** ©jet/Shutterstock **92**(top row, left to right) ©Cambridge University Press; ©Cambridge University Press; ©Cambridge University Press; ©Thinkstock; ©Cambridge University Press *(top middle row, left to right)* ©Ryan McVay/Thinkstock; ©Valentyn Volkov/Shutterstock; ©Thinkstock; ©Cambridge University Press; ©Cambridge University Press *(bottom middle row, left to right)* ©Cambridge University Press; ©Cambridge University Press; ©Cambridge University Press; ©Cambridge University Press; ©Multiart/Shutterstock (bottom row, left to right) ©Cambridge University Press; ©Cambridge University Press; ©Cambridge University Press; ©Cambridge University Press; ©svry/Shutterstock **93** *(top to bottom)* ©Cambridge University Press; ©Thinkstock; ©Thinkstock; ©Fuse/Getty Images/RF **96** ©Lena Pantiukh/Shutterstock

Text credits

While every effort has been made, it has not always been possible to identify the sources of all the material used, or to trace all copyright holders. If any omissions are brought to our notice, we will be happy to include the appropriate acknowledgements on reprinting.

Special thanks to Kerry S. Vrabel for his editorial contributions.

The top 500 spoken words

This is a list of the top 500 words in spoken North American English. It is based on a sample of four and a half million words of conversation from the Cambridge International Corpus. The most frequent word, *I*, is at the top of the list.

1. I
2. and
3. the
4. you
5. uh
6. to
7. a
8. that
9. it
10. of
11. yeah
12. know
13. in
14. like
15. they
16. have
17. so
18. was
19. but
20. is
21. it's
22. we
23. huh
24. just
25. oh
26. do
27. don't
28. that's
29. well
30. for
31. what
32. on
33. think
34. right
35. not
36. um
37. or
38. my
39. be
40. really
41. with
42. he
43. one
44. are
45. this
46. there
47. I'm
48. all
49. if
50. no
51. get
52. about
53. at
54. out
55. had
56. then
57. because
58. go
59. up
60. she
61. when
62. them
63. can
64. would
65. as
66. me
67. mean
68. some
69. good
70. got
71. OK
72. people
73. now
74. going
75. were
76. lot
77. your
78. time
79. see
80. how
81. they're
82. kind
83. here
84. from
85. did
86. something
87. too
88. more
89. very
90. want
91. little
92. been
93. things
94. an
95. you're
96. said
97. there's
98. I've
99. much
100. where
101. two
102. thing
103. her
104. didn't
105. other
106. say
107. back
108. could
109. their
110. our
111. guess
112. yes
113. way
114. has
115. down
116. we're
117. any

118. he's
119. work
120. take
121. even
122. those
123. over
124. probably
125. him
126. who
127. put
128. years
129. sure
130. can't
131. pretty
132. gonna
133. stuff
134. come
135. these
136. by
137. into
138. went
139. make
140. than
141. year
142. three
143. which
144. home
145. will
146. nice
147. never
148. only
149. his
150. doing
151. cause
152. off
153. I'll
154. maybe
155. real
156. why
157. big
158. actually
159. she's
160. day
161. five
162. always
163. school
164. look
165. still
166. around
167. anything
168. kids
169. first
170. does
171. need
172. us
173. should
174. talking
175. last
176. thought
177. doesn't
178. different
179. money
180. long
181. used
182. getting
183. same
184. four
185. every
186. new
187. everything
188. many
189. before
190. though
191. most
192. tell
193. being
194. bit
195. house
196. also
197. use
198. through
199. feel
200. course
201. what's
202. old
203. done
204. sort
205. great
206. bad
207. we've
208. another
209. car
210. true
211. whole
212. whatever
213. twenty
214. after
215. ever
216. find
217. care
218. better
219. hard
220. haven't
221. trying
222. give
223. I'd
224. problem
225. else
226. remember
227. might
228. again
229. pay
230. try
231. place
232. part
233. let
234. keep
235. children
236. anyway
237. came
238. six
239. family
240. wasn't
241. talk
242. made
243. hundred
244. night
245. call
246. saying

247. dollars
248. live
249. away
250. either
251. read
252. having
253. far
254. watch
255. week
256. mhm
257. quite
258. enough
259. next
260. couple
261. own
262. wouldn't
263. ten
264. interesting
265. am
266. sometimes
267. bye
268. seems
269. heard
270. goes
271. called
272. point
273. ago
274. while
275. fact
276. once
277. seen
278. wanted
279. isn't
280. start
281. high
282. somebody
283. let's
284. times
285. guy
286. area
287. fun
288. they've
289. you've
290. started
291. job
292. says
293. play
294. usually
295. wow
296. exactly
297. took
298. few
299. child
300. thirty
301. buy
302. person
303. working
304. half
305. looking
306. someone
307. coming
308. eight
309. love
310. everybody
311. able
312. we'll
313. life
314. may
315. both
316. type
317. end
318. least
319. told
320. saw
321. college
322. ones
323. almost
324. since
325. days
326. couldn't
327. gets
328. guys
329. god
330. country
331. wait
332. yet
333. believe
334. thinking
335. funny
336. state
337. until
338. husband
339. idea
340. name
341. seven
342. together
343. each
344. hear
345. help
346. nothing
347. parents
348. room
349. today
350. makes
351. stay
352. mom
353. sounds
354. change
355. understand
356. such
357. gone
358. system
359. comes
360. thank
361. show
362. thousand
363. left
364. friends
365. class
366. already
367. eat
368. small
369. boy
370. paper
371. world
372. best
373. water
374. myself
375. run

376. they'll
377. won't
378. movie
379. cool
380. news
381. number
382. man
383. basically
384. nine
385. enjoy
386. bought
387. whether
388. especially
389. taking
390. sit
391. book
392. fifty
393. months
394. women
395. month
396. found
397. side
398. food
399. looks
400. summer
401. hmm
402. fine
403. hey
404. student
405. agree
406. mother
407. problems
408. city
409. second
410. definitely
411. spend
412. happened
413. hours
414. war
415. matter
416. supposed
417. worked
418. company
419. friend
420. set
421. minutes
422. morning
423. between
424. music
425. close
426. leave
427. wife
428. knew
429. pick
430. important
431. ask
432. hour
433. deal
434. mine
435. reason
436. credit
437. dog
438. group
439. turn
440. making
441. American
442. weeks
443. certain
444. less
445. must
446. dad
447. during
448. lived
449. forty
450. air
451. government
452. eighty
453. wonderful
454. seem
455. wrong
456. young
457. places
458. girl
459. happen
460. sorry
461. living
462. drive
463. outside
464. bring
465. easy
466. stop
467. percent
468. hand
469. gosh
470. top
471. cut
472. computer
473. tried
474. gotten
475. mind
476. business
477. anybody
478. takes
479. aren't
480. question
481. rather
482. twelve
483. phone
484. program
485. without
486. moved
487. gave
488. yep
489. case
490. looked
491. certainly
492. talked
493. beautiful
494. card
495. walk
496. married
497. anymore
498. you'll
499. middle
500. tax